ISBN 978-0-365-40168-1
PIBN 10826349

HA MONIC COMPANION,

AND

GUIDE TO SOCIAL WORSHIP:

BEING

A CHOICE SELECTION OF TUNES,

adapted to the various Psalms and Hymns, used by the different Societies in the United States;
TOGETHER WITH THE PRINCIPLES OF MUSIC, AND EASY LESSONS FOR LEARNERS.

By ANDREW LAW.

PRINTED UPON THE AUTHOR'S NEW PLAN.

PHILADELPHIA.....PUBLISHED BY THE AUTHOR, and DAVID HOGAN, No. 51, S. THIRD STREET.

FROM THE PRESS OF THOMAS T. STILES.

DEDICATION.

THE MINISTERS OF THE GOSPEL, AND THE SINGING MASTERS, CLERKS AND CHORISTERS THROUGHOUT THE UNITED STATES.

ENTLEMEN,

    THE following work is addressed to you. It claims your candid and thorough perusal. It exhibits an oductory Treatise and an Elementary Scale, possessing, it is believed, improvements of real and permanent th; and it also presents specimens of that chaste and sober, that sublime and solemn Psalmody, which the ds of religion and virtue, as well as the friends of sacred song, would rejoice to see more generally improv- worshipping assemblies.

    It will not, perhaps, have escaped the observation of any one of you, that very much of the music in vogue is rable indeed. Hence the man of piety and principle, of taste and discernment in music, and hence, indeed, all, entertain a sense of decency and decorum in devotion, are oftentimes offended with that lifeless and insipid, or frivolous and frolicksome succession and combination of sounds, so frequently introduced into churches, where all ld be serious, animated and devout; and hence the dignity and the ever varying vigor of Handel, of Madan, of others, alike meritorious, are, in a great measure, supplanted by the pitiful productions of numerous compo-, whom it would be doing too much honor to name. Let any one acquainted with the sublime and beautiful ositions of the great Masters of Music, but look round within the circle of his own acquaintance, and he will abundant reason for these remarks.

4

The evil is obvious. Much of the predominating Psalmody of this country is more like song singing, than solemn praise. It rests with you, Gentlemen, to apply the remedy. The work of reformation is arduous, but impracticable, and the more difficult the task, the more praise worthy the accomplishment.

I will further add, that there are no description of citizens in the community, who have it in their power do half as much, as you, towards correcting and perfecting the taste in music, and towards giving to devotio praise its due effect upon our lives and conversation.

The cause of religion and virtue has therefore a claim upon your exertions. What remains then, but every one who is convinced of the want, begin the work? Individual exertions, rendered unexceptionable, bec universal, and the business is ended.

That you may criticise with the keenness and candor of real masters of music, and correct with the courage conduct of irresistible reformers, is all that the fondest friends of sacred music would ask or wish; and if the lowing Book be found but an individual's mite towards promoting so noble an undertaking, as that of impro- the religious praise of a rising Empire, it will never become a subject of regret to one, who has devoted greater part of his life to the cultivation of Psalmody, and who is,

With all proper Respects,

THE AUTHOR.

PREFACE.

N compiling the following work, or the Harmonic Companion, I have endeavoured to compose an elementary system which might open, e, an improved pathway to the practice of music. I could not be at a loss in supposing, that such an acquisition would be very accept-) all classes of singers, and especially to those on whom the business of teaching devolves, as well as to all learners, during the first of their progress. To encompass my object, I have withheld no improvements, which patient industry, aided by more than twenty experience in studying and teaching vocal music, could bestow ; and I flatter myself, than the friends of Psalmody will find my Harmo- mpanion, an easier, and more eligible Book for beginners, than any one that has heretofore appeared.

he Introductory Treatise immediately following, a number of the most important things relating to vocal music, are concisely explain- l clearly enforced.

it is the Scale of Rules with which the labor, the actual task of the learner, more immediately commences. To render this task as ea-)ossible, neither time nor attention have been spared. As the readiest way to effect the purpose proposed, appeal has been uniformly to the reason and nature of my subject, as presented in theory and practice. For the scale which follows, is not the offspring of a short and y attention to theory alone. On the contrary, it forms the result of those gradual improvements produced by repeated reflection and re- d trials in the school of experience. European Gamuts in the mean while have not been overlooked. On the other hand, I have ever ned them with care and deference ; but at the same time, without thinking myself obliged to be implicitly guided by them, merely, be- they were already in use. For a thousand things are in use, which ought not to be copied. Hence, wherever I have discovered, that al- ps might be made for the better, I have not scrupled to introduce them.

music is not, at present, printed upon this Plan, and according to the Rules of this Scale ; but all music might be thus printed, and t very means, be improved in point of simplicity. In regard to the music which is contained in the Harmonic Companion, the rules are thrown out of this system, are not wanted ; and as to any other music, it may, in all cases, be rendered more simple, by transcrib- into the Plan of this Scale. If any one should, however, choose to consult other music, as it stands, he will find the necessary direc- 4ith it. It will then be soon enough for him to attend to the rules for that purpose, when he actually finds, that he shall want them. s attending to them at such after period, will rather be an alleviation to him, than otherwise ; for he will then, probably, have fewer to distract and divide his mind, than at his first setting out. At any rate, his attending to them, later, or by themselves, can be no nal burthen to him ; for whatever is thrown out of this system, is knit into the body of common systems ; and by adverting to them, ouly advert to some old rules, which, if music were printed as it might be, would be utterly useless.

This Book exhibits a plan and method which are different from any that have yet appeared.

The principal objects of this plan and of this method, are to lessen the burden of the learner; to facilitate the performance, or pr of Music; and to promote a general improvement in the praises of our God and Redeemer.

Three of the musical characters are made more simple by rejecting the long stroke of the crotchet, which is one half of the characte this means the parts of the quaver are diminished one third; and those of the semi-quaver one fourth. The cliffs, F and G, and the r R, being characters used as letters, are familiar to every one; these are used instead of those which are unknown, till learned as m characters. The four kinds of characters denote the four singing syllables; and the learner will immediately name the notes with gr cility, and will read them with equal ease in every part, and in all the different changes of the keys. But these are not the greatest a tages derived from the plan, and the method of teaching by these characters.

Music, printed without the lines, is more simple than it can be on lines and spaces; because the lines and spaces increase the num the parts which compose the characters, and render them more indistinct, and more difficult to be retained in the memory. This pla assist, both the learner and the performer, in ascertaining the true sounds of the notes in instances where the old method cannot affo aid for that purpose.

The music is taught in this method by the degrees of the keys, and the common chord taken upon the key note, or first degree of th Lessons of these are given in the Scale of Rules.

There are only two keys in music, the sharp, or major key; and the flat, or minor key. There are also only two common chords upon the key note, or first degree of the key; one for the sharp key, and one for the flat key, and these chords differ only in the thi gree, which is half a tone higher in the sharp, than in the flat key.

These keys and common chords have their particular characters for each degree, which are fixed invariably; and when ever the shifted, from one letter to another, the characters and the common chord are shifted with the key; and retain, from the key note, the order of characters, of names, and of arrangement of tones, and semitones. Hence, this method marks, with certainty, the intervals, or dis of sounds. The places of the tones and semitones, the major and minor seconds, thirds and fourths, are always in view. The semito between the diamond and the square, and the quarter of a diamond and the square. Hence, when any two notes are placed at the dist a second, a third, or a fourth, it will instantly appear from the sight of the characters, whether the interval be the major, or the minor third, or fourth. This is an advantage which the old method can never possess; for it cannot be known from the common notes upo and spaces whether these intervals be major, or minor; only by referring back to the cliffs; but in this method it is visible in every b

diamond note is never double in the same octave. It is fixed between the two keys, and is the seventh degree of sharp key, and the degree of the flat key. The quarter of a diamond and the square which immediately succeed each other in ascending, or in descend-, the third and fourth degrees of the sharp key, and the fifth and six degrees of the flat key. And, from this view of the method, it be difficult to ascertain the degrees of the keys; for if any one degree be found, all the others will follow of course. The last note ass is always the square in the sharp key, and the quarter of a diamond in the flat key. Therefore by looking at the last note of the d then at a few bars of a tune, either the diamond, or the quarter of a diamond and the square, together, will appear, by which the i degree, or the third and fourth of the sharp key will be known; and the second degree, or the fifth and sixth of the flat key.
similarity of the characters, of the names of the notes, and of the order of the tones and semitones, in every part of the music, and in different changes of the keys, render the business of the learner very simple and easy; and will greatly diminish the expenses of tui-d the consumption of time necessarily employed in learning the Art. By this method children will soon learn to read music as easi-ey read other books. And those who practise upon this method will find the burden of the performance greatly alleviated, and be able any part that is within the compass of their voices.
 this view of the subject, is it not rational to suppose, that great advantages may be derived from the introduction of this plan? Upon n and method the knowledge of the Art will be easily obtained; and music will be read in a short time with great facility. The na-nsequence of this will be, that the cultivation of the Art will become more general; and the practice of it will be rendered more plea-d entertaining.

N O T E S.

IE tunes, Gath, Lebanon, Miletus, Transport, and Glocester, may be sung as long metres, or as the metre of six lines, all The tune Leoni may be sung as a short metre, by dividing each of the two middle notes of every fourth line, into two notes; nto two minims, or into a dotted minim and crotchet. Cadiz may be sung to the metre of Amsterdam, by adding a slur to the two es of the sixth line.
e first part of the Funeral Piece is to be sung in the three verses which are set to it, before the other part is sung.
nes which require the repetition of some words, will, in some instances, require a different repetition; as in Hotham, the second With the shadow;" this may be done by throwing out the slur.
nes with a Chorus; the chorus may be sung after every verse, after the last verse only, or omitted entirely.
those parts of tunes, over which the word Unisons is placed, all sing the same part.
 first part of Amsterdam is repeated in the third and fourth lines of each verse.

TONING AND TUNING THE VOICE.

GOOD tones, in proper tune, are indispensibly requisite in order to good music. One of the first and most important objects o Instructor, should therefore be, to modulate the tones, or sounds of each voice, so as to render them agreeable; and where different v join together, with a design of producing harmony, they should all take the same pitch and move in perfect tune. The tones of the hu voice, in order to be agreeable, must be open, smooth and flexible; and, to be in tune, each voice must accord with the others.

ARTICULATION AND PRONUNCIATION.

Words and Syllables, as far as music will admit, ought to be articulated and pronounced according to the true standard of conversa But in aiming at this point, care must be taken, not to injure the sounds of the music. Syllables must be articulated at their begin or ending, or at both, according as they are begun or ended with vowels or consonants; and in dwelling upon a syllable between its b ning and end, the voice must open, swell and expand. And in this way, agreeable sounds may be preserved; whereas, without such op of the voice, flat and disagreeable sounds will frequently ensue.

In practising vocal music by note, the syllables, mi, faw, sol, law, are used, as the vehicles of sound. These, properly pronoun are admirably calculated for the purpose to which they are appropriated They assist in forming the organs of speech, into positions pr for making the tones open, soft and smooth. There true pronunciation is easy, the i, in mi, has its short sound, as in divinity; the. sol, has its long sound, as in sold; and the faw and law are pronounced as written.

THE PARTS.

The Bass is properly considered as the ground work, or foundation. Correct Composers of modern date, for the most part, mak of treble, as the leading part, or air; and this appears most agreeable to the principles of harmony, which incline to ascribe the Melody, or song to the treble; while the tenor and counter, or second treble, come in to fill up and perfect the harmony. Where r consists of four parts, that which is written lowest is Bass; the next above it is the Tenor; then the Counter, or second Treble; and a top, the Treble. REMARK. Whenever tunes are performed only in two parts, they should be sung in the Bass and the air, or prin melody; and in such cases, they may be sung either by Tenor or Treble voices, or by both of them united.

THE CLIFFS.

I have used only two cliffs; the F, or Bass cliff, and the ;, or treble cliff, which answers alike for Treble, Counter and Tenor. Counter is transposed to the octave, or eighth below. The notes being thus transposed, they are sung in the Treble voice.

SHARPS AND FLATS.

In every octave, or regular succession of eight notes, ascending or descending, there are five whole tones, and two half or semi In their natural order, the semitones are fixed between B and C; and E and F. Between mi and faw, and law and faw. For the s variety, it becomes necessary to shift the order of the semitones. This is done by flats and sharps. The first sharp is placed on second on C, the third on G, and the fourth on D. The first flat is on B, the second on E, the third on A, and the fourth on D.

ACCENT.

A greater stress of voice upon any particular part of the bar is what is called Accent. Singers in performing single common and ple time, should be careful to accent only that part of the bar, which is marked by the first beat; and in performing double common ne, they should place a full accent upon that part of the bar, which is marked by the first beat, and only a half accent upon that part, which marked by the third beat.

THE SWELL.

The swell is in one sense applicable to all music. There is something of it upon every note, or syllable that is sung. In quantity it in degree proportioned to the length of the note, and is formed by increasing the sound to the middle of the note, and decreasing it to : close.

OF SOFT AND LOUD.

Softness and loudness are to music what light and shade are to painting. While the voice is very soft and small, the sentiments ex-essed, are wrapt in deep shade, and seen at a distance; but when the music increases in loudness to the extent of the human voice, the itiments are seen hastening from the shade, and advancing into a glare of light; and when soft singing again succeeds, they again retire, l discover themselves beneath the dim and distant shades. To sing, sometimes loud, at others soft, as the sentiments require, is indeed rincipal beauty of singing. By this means objects appear in the blaze of day, in the shade, or in the twilight, at the performers bidding; ile to the music is added, variety and richness of expression, and oftentimes a more than double effect.

TIME.

Time in music is originally of two kinds, Common and Triple. These are distinguished from each other by the different divisions he bar into its primary or principal parts. Whenever the bar is in the very first instance, divided into an even number of parts, the music n Common time; but if divided into an uneven number of parts, the music is in Triple time. In Triple time, the bar is always divided three parts, and marked by three beats. In Common time, it is sometimes, divided into four parts, and marked by four beats; but e generally into two parts only, and marked by two beats.

MODES.

The Modes depend upon the movement of the music. As long as that moves uniformly fast or slow, the mode continues the same; but e music either quicken or slaken its movement, the mode changes. In the scale I have distinguished the Modes to the number of seven. se belong alike to each kind of time, and are known, as occasion requires, by placing the name of the mode over the music, where the movement begins.

B

CHARACTERS.	EXPLANATIONS.

Four kinds of characters, to wit, ◇ ☐ ○ ◣ . The diamond is mi ; the square is faw ; the round is sol ; and the quarter of a diamond is law.

Notes or marks of sounds.	Rests or marks of silence.

mi faw sol law

Breves	Breve Rest
Semibreves	Semibreve
Minims	Minim
Crotchets	Crotchet
Quavers	Quaver
Semiquavers	

Proportion of the Notes.

One ◣ Breve is

Two ☐ ○ Semibreves,

Four Minims,

Eight Crotchets,

Sixteen Quavers,

Thirty two Semiquavers.

The rests have the same proportion except the semibreve, which fills a bar in Triple time.

Brace (Shows how many parts are sung together.

Cliff G Is used in Treble, Counter and Tenor.
Cliff F Is used in Bass only.

Close ||| Shows the end of the Tune.

Slur ⌒ Shows what notes are sung to one syllable.

Dot . At the right hand of a note, adds to it half its length.

Figure 3 Shows that each of the three notes is one third of a beat.

Single bar | Divides the time according to the measure note.

Double notes Either may be sung.

Double bar || Shows when to repeat.

Repeat R Shows that the tune is sung again from that note to a double bar or close.

Figures 1, 2, Show that the note under 1, is sung the first time, and that under 2, the second time.

Preparative or leaning notes ⬤○. These notes add nothing to the time of bar in which they are used, for whatever time be occupied by them, so mu must be taken from the notes with which they are connected.

IRISH. C. M.

Awake my heart, arise my tongue, Prepare a tuneful voice, In God, the life of all my joys Aloud will I rejoice.

BOLTON. L. M.

Bless, O my soul, the living God: Call home thy thoughts that rove abroad, Let all the powers within me join In work and worship so divine.

BEDFORD. C. M.

16 Cheerful.

Awake ye saints, to praise your king, Your sweetest passions raise ; Your pious pleasure, while

SUTTON. S. M.

Moderate.

Oh bless the Lord, my soul, Let all with · in me join, And aid my tongue to bless his

In every flat key, the first and fifth degrees, are the quarter of a diamond figure ; the second degree, is the diamond; the third and sixth grees, are the square ; and the fourth and seventh degrees, are the round.

The diamond note is never double in the same octave. It is the second degree of the flat key. The quarter of a diamond and the are which immediately succeed each other, the square a little higher than the quarter of a diamond, are the fifth and sixth degrees of : flat key.

Flat key of A.   Common Chord, A, C, E,   Flat key of D, D, F, A.   LESSON IX.

st degree	A
venth degree	G
th degree	F
th degree	E
urth degree	D
iird degree	C
cond degree	B
rst degree	A

Moderate.   DUBLIN. C. M.

With earnest longings of the mind.   My God, to thee I look;   So pants the hunted hart, to find,   And taste the cool - ing brook.

C

Moderate.

AYLESBURY. S. M.

I lift my soul to God, My trust is in his name; Let not my foes that seek my blood Still triumph in m

Slow.

GROTON. L. M.

Deep in our hearts let us record The deeper sorrows of our Lord; Behold the rising billows roll To overwhelm his hol

Moderate.

Man has a soul of vast desires; He burns within with restless fires; Tost to and fro his passions fly From van - i - ty to

Cheerful.   COVENTRY. S. M.

n - i - ty.   Lord, what a fee - - ble piece is this our mortal frame! Our life how poor a tri-fle 'tis, That scarce deserves the name!

BLOOMFIELD. S. M.

Cheerful.

My God per - mit my tongue This joy, to call thee mine : And let my early cries prevail, To taste thy love di - vine.

Moderate.

GEORGIA. C. M.

Return, O God of love, return, Earth is a tiresome place ; How long shall we thy children mourn Our absence from thy f

BETHLEHEM. S. M.

lof - ty sky declares its mak - er God, And all the star - ry works on high Proclaim his power aboard.

LITCHFIELD. L. M.

s my Saviour speaks! How kind the promises he makes! A bruised reed he never breaks Nor will he quench the smoking flax,

Soft. DUNSTAN. L. M. Loud.

Jesus shall reign where'er the sun Does his successive journeys run; His kingdom stretch from shore to shore, Till moons shall wax and wane no more. Till moons, shall w

PORTUGAL. L. M.

Behold the rose of Sharon here, The lily which the vallies bear; Behold the tree of life; that gives Refreshing fruit and healing leave

SURRY. L. M.

O come loud anthems let us sing, Loud thanks to our Almighty King; For we our voices high should raise, When our salvation's rock we praise.

WAKEFIELD. C. M.

To cel-e-brate thy praise, O Lord, I will my heart prepare; To all the listening world thy works, Thy wondrous works declare.

24   Cheerful.

NEW LONDON. L. M.

What is our God, or what his name: Nor men can learn, nor an - gels teach: He dwells conceal'd in radiant flame, Where neither

eyes nor thoughts can reach.

Cheerful.   COLCHESTER. C. M.

My soul, how lovely is the place To which thy God resorts! 'Tis heaven to see his smiling face, Tho' 'tis his earthly co

Moderate.

Give thanks to God moſt high, The un - i - ver - ſal Lord! The ſovereign King of kings; And be his grace ador'd.　His power and grace are ſtill the ſame; And

Moderate.　READING. C. M.

is name have endleſs praiſe.　Bleſt are the ſouls that hear and know The goſpel's joyful ſound! Peace ſhall attend the path they go, And light their steps ſurround.

D

26 Cheerful.

Lord of the worlds above, How pleasant and how fair The dwellings of thy love, Thine earthly temples are ! To thine abode

Moderate.   GATH. L. M.

Soft.   Loud.

pires, With warm desires, To see my God, With warm desires, To see my God.

He reigns the Lord, the Sav - iour reigns ! Praise him in

van - gel - ic ſtrains;   Let the whole earth in ſongs rejoice,   And diſtant iſlands join their voice,   And dis - tant iſlands join their voice.

LEEDS.   L. M.

and righteouſneſs My beauty are my glorious dreſs,   'Midſt flaming worlds in theſe array'd,   With joy ſhall I lift up my head.

GERMANY. S. M.

28 Moderate.

Sing to the Lord aloud, sing to the Lord aloud, And make a joyful noise, and make a joyful noise; God is our strength, our Saviour God

Israel hear his voice.

EASTON. C. M.

Moderate.

That awful day will surely come, The appointed hour makes haste, When I must stand before my judge, And pass the sol

NESTON. L. M.

Moderate.

Why should we start and fear to die? What tim'rous worms we mortals are! Death is the gate of endless joy, And yet we dread to enter there.

SCOTLAND. L. M.

Moderate.

Ere long the awful day shall come, When Christ in glory shall appear, And all the world their final doom, From his most righteous lips must hear.

SUNDERLAND. P. M.

30 Cheerful.

Let all the earth their voices raise, To sing the choicest pfalm of praife, To fing and blefs Jehovah's name ; His glory let the heathen know, His won

to the nations fhow,   And all his faving works proclaim,

Cheerful.   CHARLESTON. P. M.

I'll praife my Maker with my breath ;   And when my voice is h, Praife fhall employ my nobler powers; My days of praife fhall ne'er be paft While life, and thought, and being laft, Or im‑mor‑tal‑i‑ty endures.

Moderate.   HADDAM. S. M.

When overwhelm'd with grief, My heart within me dies ; Helpless and far from all re‑lief, To heaven I lift my eyes.

HANOVER. Pec. M.

O praise ye the Lord, prepare your glad voice, His praise in the great assembly to sing. In out great Creator let Israel rejoice: And children of Zion be

Cheerful.

MANSFEILD. S. M.

glad in their king.   The darkness and the light Still keep their course same; While night to day, and day to night Divine- ly teach his name.

When God reveal'd his gracious name, And chang'd my mournful state, My rapture seem'd a pleasant dream, The grace appear'd so great. The world beheld the

glorious change, And did thy hand confess; My tongue broke out in unknown strains, And sung surprising grace, My tongue broke out in unknown strains, And sung surprising grace.

84 Moderate.

Soon as I heard my Father fay, Ye children, feek my grace,

My heart re-

My heart reply'd with-out delay, I'll feek my Father's face.

Cheerful. PELHAM. S. M.

ply'd with-out   delay, I'll feek my Father's face.

My foul repeat his praife, Whofe mercies are fo great ; Whofe anger is fo flow to rife, So   rea-dy

soft.   Loud.   Soft.   Loud.

to abate, High as the heavens are rais'd   Above the ground we tread, So far the riches of his grace Our highest thoughts exceed, Our highest thoughts exceed.

Unisons.

Moderate.   BURFORD. C. M.

My soul come med-i-tate the day, And think how near it stands, When thou must quit this house of clay, And fly to unknown lands.

NAPLES. C. M.

Moderate.

Soft.

Loud.

There is a fountain fill'd with blood, Drawn from Immanuel's veins, And sinners plung'd beneath that flood Lose all their guilty stains. And

Cheerful.

CANTON. P. M.

sinners plung'd beneath that flood Lose all their guilty stains,

How plea - sant 'tis to see Kindred and friends agree, Each in his pro - per, station move, And each fulfil his part With sympathising heart, In all the cares of life and love, In all the cares of life and love.

Moderate. HAMBURGH. S. M.

1 Come, found his praife abroad, And hymns of glory fing. Je-ho'-vah is   the fovereign God, The uni - ver - fal King, The uni - ver - fal King.

Moderate.

CARR'S LANE. C. M.

Soft.   Loud.

G♭♭ 3/2

And does the kind Redeemer stoop, In such re - viv - ing strains, Dif - eaf - ed fin - ners to invite And heal their heart felt pains, And

G♭♭ 3/2

F♭♭ 3/2

F♭♭ 3/2

Cheerful.   WHITFIELD. S. M.

heal their heart felt pains?   Come, ye that love the Lord, And let your joys be known; Join in a fong with fweet accord, And thus furround the throne.

Cheerful.

1 Salvation! Oh, the joyful sound! 'Tis pleasure to our ears; A sovereign balm for every wound, A cordial for our fears.

3. Savation! Let the echo fly The spacious earth around, While all the armies of the sky Conspire to raise the sound.

Moderate & soft. Cheerful & loud.

2 Bury'd in sorrow, and in sin, At hell's dark door we lay; But we a - rise, by grace divine, To see a heavenly day.

2 Bury'd in sorrow, and in sin, At hell's dark door we lay; But we a - rise, by grace divine, To see a heavenly day.

Moderate. WALSAL. C. M.

Alas! and did my Saviour bleed, And did my Sovereign die! Would he devote that sacred head To such a worm as I?

Moderate. BANGOR. C. M.

Hark! from the the tombs a doleful sound, My ears attend the cry; Ye living men come view the ground, Where you must shortly lie.

Moderate.

FALMOUTH. P. M.

1. Lord, we come before thee now, At thy feet we humbly bow; Oh! do not our suit disdain; Shall we seek thee, Lord, in vain? Lord, on

2. In thine own appointed way, Now we seek thee, here we stay; Lord we know not how to go Till a blessing thou bestow. Send some

3. Comfort those who weep and mourn, Let the time of joy return; Those who are cast down, lift up; Make them strong in faith and hope. Grant that

Loud.　　　　　Soft.　　　　Loud.

thee our souls depend, In compassion now descend; Fill our hearts with thy rich grace, Tune our lips to sing thy praise, Tune our lips to sing thy praise.

message from thy word, That may joy and peace afford; Let thy spirit now impart Full salvation to each heart, Full salvation to each heart.

those who seek, may find Thee a gracious God and kind; Heal the sick, the captive free, Let us all rejoice in thee, Let us all rejoice in thee.

WASHINGTON. C.M.

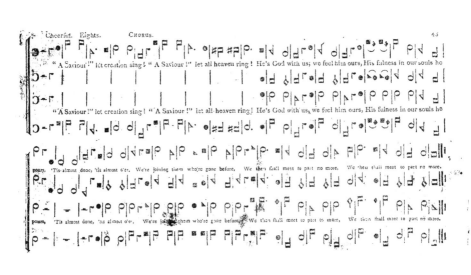

Cheerful. Eights. Chorus.

"A Saviour!" let creation sing! "A Saviour!" let all heaven ring! He's God with us; we feel him ours, His fulness in our souls he

"A Saviour!" let creation sing! "A Saviour!" let all heaven ring! He's God with us, we feel him ours, His fulness in our souls he

pours, 'Tis almost done, 'tis almost o'er, We're joining them who're gone before, We then shall meet to part no more, We then shall meet to part no more.

pours, 'Tis almost done, 'tis almost o'er, We're joining them who're gone before, We then shall meet to part no more, We then shall meet to part no more.

46 Moderate.

1. Jesu, lover of my soul, Let me to thy bosom fly; While the near-er waters roll, While the tempest still is high. Hide me, O my

2. Other refuge have I none; Hangs my helpless soul on Thee; Leave, ah! leave me not alone, Still support and comfort me. All my trust on

3. Thou, O Christ, art all I want; More than all in thee I find; Raise the fallen, cheer the faint, Heal the sick, and lead the blind. Just and holy

Soft. Loud.

Sa-viour, hide, Till the storm of life is past; Safe in-to the haven guide, O re-ceive, O re-ceive, O receive my soul at last.

thee is stay'd, All my help from thee I bring; Cover my de-fence-less head With the shadow, with the shadow With the shadow of thy wings.

is thy name; I am all un-righteous-ness! Vile, and full of sin I am, Thou art full, thou art full, Thou art full of truth and grace.

Cheerful.

1. Love divine, all love excelling, Joy of heaven, to earth come down! Fix in us thy humble dwelling, All thy faithful · mercies

2. Breathe, O breathe thy loving spirit, Into every troubled breast! Let us all in thee inherit, Let us find thy promis'd

3. Come, almighty to deliver, Let us all thy life receive! Suddenly return, and never, Never more thy temples

crown, Jesus! thou art all compassion, Pure, unbounded love thou art; Visit us with thy salvation, Enter every trembling heart!

rest. Take away the love of sinning, Alpha and Om · e · ga be, End of faith as its beginning, Set our hearts at li · ber · ty.

leave! Thee we would be always blessing, Serve thee as thine hosts above; Pray, and praise thee without ceasing; Glory in thy precious love!

ITALY. C. M.

48 Moderate.

Let him embrace my soul, and prove Mine int'rest in his heavenly love; The voice which tells me, thou art mine, Exceeds the blessings of the vine. On thee the ae-

Soft.   Loud.

cinding Spirit came, And spreads the favour of thy name; That oil of gladness and of grace Draws holy souls to meet thy face, Draws holy souls to meet thy face.

Moderate. Soft.   Loud.   Soft.

1. The righteous fouls that take their flight Far from this world of pain, In God's pa - ter - nal bofom blest For ever shall re - main.

2. To minds unwise they feem to die, All joyful hopes to ceafe; Yet they, fecur'd by Je - fus, live In ev - er - laft - ing peace.

3. And at the great, the awful day, When Chrift defcends from high, With myriads of triumphant faints, He'll own them in the fky.

Moderate. Loud.   Diminifh.   Loud.

4. Then He, their Judge, their mighty Lord, Difplays re - deeming grace, And calls them ev - er to behold, The brightnefs of his face.

4. Then He, their Judge, their mighty Lord, Difplays re - deeming grace, And calls them ev - er to behold, The brightnefs of his face.

G

CADIZ. P. M. Eights.

1. Je - fus, let thy pitying eye Call back a wand'ring sheep; False to thee like Pe - - ter, I would fain like Pe - ter, weep.

2. Sa - viour, Prince, enthron'd above, Re - pent - ance to im - part, Give me, through thy dy - ing love, The humble contrite heart.

3. See me, Saviour, from above, Nor suffer me to die. Life and hap - pi - nefs, and love, Drop from thy gracious eye.

Let me be by grace restor'd, On me be all long fuff - 'ring shown; Turn, and look up - on me, Lord, And break my heart of stone.

Give, what I have long implor'd, A portion of thy grief unknown: Turn, and look up - on me, Lord, And break my heart of stone.

Speak the rec - on - cil - ing word, And let thy mer - cy melt me down: Turn, and look up - on me, Lord, And break my heart of stone.

ATHENS. C. M.

Slow.   Soft.   Loud.

And will the Lord thus con - de - fcend To vif - it fin - ful worms? Thus at the door fhall mer - cy ftand, in all her winning

Unisons.   Soft.

forms. Sur - priz - ing grace! and fhall my heart Unmov'd and cold remain? Has this hard rock no ten - der part? Muft mer - cy plead in vain?

Moderate.

PORTLAND. S. M.

My Maker and my King! To thee my all I owe; Thy sov'reign bounty is the spring From which my blessings flow. Thou ever, ever

Soft. Loud.

good and kind A thousand, thousand reasons move; A thousand ob - li - gations bind, A thousand ob - li - gations bind, My heart to grateful love.

CONCORD. L. M.

Moderate.

O God how free thy mer-cies flow, But thy re-luct-ant wrath how flow! High as the bright ex-pand-ed

fkies, Thy vaft unbound-ed mer-cies rife. High as the bright ex-pand-ed fkies, Thy vaft un-bound-ed mercies rife.

LEBANON. L. M. or as the 113th. Psalm.

Moderate.

1. Father of all, omnifcient mind, Thy wifdom who can comprehend? Its higheft point what eye can find; Or to its low - eft depths defcend?

2. What cavern deep, what hill fublime, Beyond thy reach, fhall I purfue? What dark recefs, what diftant clime, Shall hide me from thy boundlefs view?

Its higheft point, what eye can find: Or to its loweft depths defcend?

What dark recefs, what diftant clime, Shall hide me from thy boundlefs view?

Cheerful. WINCHESTER. Pec. M.

1. Lo! He cometh! count - lefs trumpets Blow to raife the fleep-ing dead;

2. Now his mer - its, by the harpers Thro' th' e - ter - nal deep refounds;

Soft. Loud. 55

'Midft ten thoufand faints and an-gels, See, their great ex-alt-ed head! Hal-le-lu-jah, hal-le-lu-jah, Welcome, welcome Son of God,

Now re-fplen-dent fhine his nail prints, Every eye shall fee his wound; They who pierc'd him, they who pierc'd him Shall, at his ap-pear-ance, wail.

Cheerful. Unisons. TRINITY. Pec. M.

1. Come, thou Almighty King, Help us thy name to fing: Help us to praife! Father all glorious, O'er all vic-to-ri-ous, Come and reign o'ver us, Ancient of days.

2. Jefus our Lord, arife, Scatter our en-e-mies, And make them fall! Let thine almighty aid Our fure defence be made, Our fouls on thee be ftay'd. Lord hear our call.

5. To the great One in Three Eternal praifes be, Hence—evermore! His fov'reign Majefty May we in glory fee, And to e-ter-ni-ty, Love and adore.

56 Cheerful. ASHLEY. C. M. Soft. Loud.

To our Redeemer's glorious name, Awake the sa - cred song! O may his love, (im - mor - tal flame!) Tune every heart and tongue

CHORUS. Soft. Loud.

Glory, honor, praise and power Be unto the Lamb for ever. Jesus Christ is our Re - deem - er hal - le - lu - jah, hal - le - lu - jah, hal - le - lu - jah, Praise the Lord.

Halle - lujah, halle - lu - jah, hal - le - lu - jah, Praise the Lord.

Cheerful.

ISLINGTON. L. M.

E - ter - nal source of eve - ry joy, Well may thy praise our lips employ, While in thy temple we appear, Whose goodness crowns, whose goodness crowns the circling year.

Moderate.

SICILY. C. M.

Jesus, with all thy saints above, My tongue would bear her part; Would found aloud thy saving love, And sing thy bleeding heart.

H

VIENNA. P. M.

1. World, adieu! thou re - al cheat, Oft have thy de - ceit - ful charms Fill'd my heart with fond conceit, Fool - ifh hopes and falfe a - larms.

2. Vain thy en - ter - tain - ing fights, Falfe thy prom - is - es renew'd, All the pomp of thy delights Does but flat - ter and de - lude.

CHAPEL. P. M.

Now I fee, as clear as day, How thy follies pafs a - way.

1. O love di - vine how fweet thou art! When fhall I find my willing heart A

Thee I quit for heav'n above, Object of the no - bleft love.

2. Stronger his love than death and hell; Its rich - es are unfearch - a - ble; T

ta - ken up with thee! I thirst, and faint, and die to prove, The greatness of re - deem - ing love, The love of Christ to me, The love of Christ to me.

first born sons of light Desire in vain its depths to see, They cannot reach the mystery, The length, and breadth, and height, The length, and breadth, and height.

Moderate.

CAMBRIDGE. C. M.

Jesus, I love thy charming name, 'Tis music to mine ear; Fain would I found it out so loud, That earth and heaven may hear, That earth That earth and heaven

KEDRON. Pec. M.

1. Thou sweet glid - ing Kedron, by thy silver stream, Our Saviour at midnight, when Cynthia's pale beam, Shone bright on the waters, would

2. How damp were the vapours that fell on his head, How hard was his pil - low, how hum - ble his bed, The angels a - stonish'd, grew

3. O garden of Ol - iv - et, dear honor'd spot, The fame of thy wonders shall ne'er be for - got, The theme most transport - ing to

Soft.

frequent - ly stray, And lose in thy murmurs, and lose in thy murmurs, the toils of the day, the toils of the day, the toils of the day.

sad at the fight, And follow'd their Master, and follow'd their Master, with solemn delight, with solemn de - light, with solemn de - light.

seraphs a - bove, The triumph of sorrow, the triumph of sorrow, the triumph of love, the triumph of love, the triumph of love.

Come faints, and adore him, come bow at his feet: O! give him the glory, the praise that is meet: Let joy-ful ho-san-na's un-ceasing a-

Come faints, and adore him, come bow at his feet; O! give him the glory, the praise that is meet: Let joy-ful ho-san-na's un-ceasing a-

rife, Let joyful ho-sanna's un-ceasing arise, And join the full chorus that gladdens the skies, And join the full chorus that gladdens the skies.

rife, Let joyful ho-sanna's un-ceasing arise, And join the full chorus that gladdens the skies, And join the full chorus that gladdens the skies.

TURIN. P. M. Soft. Loud. Soft.

1. Son of God! thy blessing grant, Still supply my eve-ry want; Tree of life, thine influ-ence shed, With thy sap my spir-it feed, With thy sap my

2. Tend'rest branch, a-las! am I, Wither without thee and die; Weak as helpless in-fan-cy, O confirm my soul in thee, O confirm my

Loud. Moderate. MALTA. Pec. M.

spirit feed, With thy sap my spirit feed. 1. Come, Lord, from above, The mountains remove; O'erturn all that hinders the course of thy love; My

soul in thee, O confirm my soul in thee. 2. I languish and pine For comfort divine, O when shall I say, "my be-lov-ed is mine?" I

Soft.   Loud.

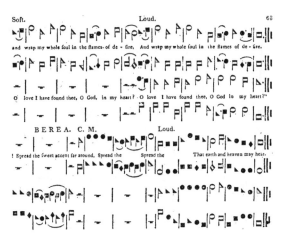

and wrap my whole soul in the flames of de - fire, And wrap my whole soul in the flames of de - fire.

O love I have found thee, O God, in my heart? O love I have found thee, O God in my heart?"

BEREA. C. M.   Loud.

! Spread the sweet accent far around, Spread the   Spread the   That earth and heaven may hear.

GALILEE. Pec. M.

1. Come and let us ascend, My companion and friend; To a taste of the banquet above; If thy heart be as mine, If for Je-sus it pine, Come up into the chariot of love, Come up into the chariot of love.

2. Who in Jesus confide, They are bold to outride All the storms of affliction beneath, With the Prophet they soar To that heavenly shore, And outfly all the arrows of death, And outfly all the arrows of death.

MILL VILLE. Pec. M.

1. Come let us anew, Our journey pursue; With vigour a - - rise, And press to our permanent place in the skie

3. At Je - - sus's call, We give up our all, And still we fore - go, For Je - - sus's sake, our en-joy-ments belov

JUDEA. C.M.

NORWICH. Pec. M.

1. How firm a founda - tion, ye saints of the Lord, Is laid for your faith, in his excellent word; What more can he say then to you he hath

2. In every condition, in sickness, in health, In pover - ty's vale, or a - bounding with wealth; At home and a - broad, on the land, on the

said? You, who unto Jesus for re - fuge have fled.

Cheerful.

MARSEILLES. P. M.

1. All hail, incar - nate God! The wond'rous things foretold Of thee, in sacred

sea, "As days may demand, so thy succour shall be."

2. To thee the hoar - y head Its silver honor pays; To thee the blooming

Soft.   Loud.

writ, With joy our eyes be - hold. Still does thine arm new trophies wear, And monuments, and monuments, and mon - u - ments of glory rear.

youth Devotes his brightest days. And every age their tribute bring, And bow to thee, and bow to thee, and bow to thee, all conq'ring King.

EVENING HYMN. L. M.

Glory to thee my God this night For all the blessings of the light. Keep me, O keep me, King of kings Under thy own Almighty wings.

CALVARY. Pec. M.

1. Hark! the voice of love and mercy Sounds aloud from Calva-ry! See! it rends the rocks asun-der, Shakes the earth and veils the sky.

2. It is fin-ish'd! O what pleasure Do these charming words afford! Heavenly blessings without measure, Flow to us from Christ the Lord.

Slow and Soft   Moderate and loud.   Moderate.   LEONI. P. M.

"It is fin-ish'd! It is fin-ish'd!" Hear the dying Saviour cry.   1. The God of Abr'ham praise, Who reigns enthron'd above   Ancient of

"It is finish'd! It is finish'd!" Saints the dying words record.   5. Before the Saviour's face The ransom'd nations bow; O'erwhelm'd at

Soft. DERBY. C. M.

Cheerful. Unisons.

Praise ye the Lord, immortal choir, That fills the realms above, Praise him who form'd you of his fire, Praise him who form'd you of his fire, And feeds you with his love.

LYSTRA. P. M.

Moderate.

1. The joyful morn, my God, is come, That calls me to thy honor'd dome Thy presence to adore; thy pre - sence to adore; My feet the summons shall attend, With

2. Hither from Judah's utmost end, The heaven protected tribes ascend; Their offerings hither bring; Their off'rings hither bring; Here, eager to attest their joy, In

Soft. Loud. Moderate. MYRA. S. M.

willing steps thy courts ascend, And tread the hallow'd floor, And tread the hallow'd floor. 1. Your harps, ye trembling saints, Down from the willows take; Loud

hymns of praise their tongues employ, All hail th' immortal King, All hail th' immortal King. 2. Tho' in a foreign land, we are not far from home; And

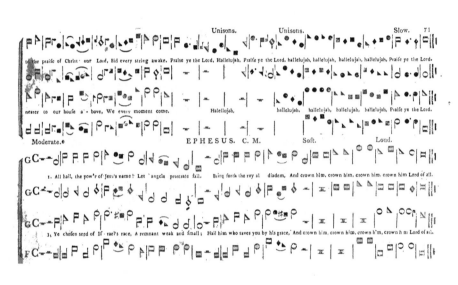

Unisons.   Unisons.   Slow.   71

to the praise of Christ our Lord, Bid every string awake. Praise ye the Lord, Hallelujah, Praise ye the Lord, hallelujah, hallelujah, hallelujah, hallelujah, Praise ye the Lord.

nearer to our house a - bove, We every moment come.   Halelllujah,   hallelujah,   hallelujah, hallelujah, hallelujah, Praise ye the Lord.

Moderate.   EPHESUS. C. M.   Soft.   Loud.

1. All hail, the pow'r of Jesu's name! Let angels prostrate fall. Bring forth the roy al diadem, And crown him, crown him, crown him, crown him Lord of all.

3. Ye chosen seed of If - rael's race, A remnant weak and small; Hail him who saves you by his grace, And crown him, crown him, crown h'm, crown him Lord of all.

PORTSMOUTH. P.M.

Soft.

Blow ye the trumpet blow ; The gladly solemn sound   Let all the nations know, Let all the nations know To earth's remotest bound.

Loud.   Soft.   Loud.

to earth's remotest bound. The year of Jubilee is come ; Return ye ransom'd sinners home, The year of Jubilee is come ; Return ye ransom'd sinners home.

Moderate. — Soft. Loud. **BRISTOL.** Pec. M. Soft.

1. Lift up your heads in joyful hope, Salute the happy morn; Salute the happy   Each heavenly power Proclaims the glad hour, Lo, Jesus the Saviour is born! Lo,

2. All glory be to God on high, To him the praise is due; To him the praise.   The promise is seal'd The Saviour's reveal'd, And proves that the record is true, And

Loud. Moderate. **WINDSOR.** C. M.

Jesus the Saviour is born.   1. Death! what a solemn word to all! What mortal things are men! We just arise and soon we fall, To mix with earth again.

proves that the record is true.   5. Oh! fit us for thy soverign will, Thy mercy, Lord, impart; Help us thy pleasure to fulfil, And yield thee all our heart.

K

TEMPEST. Pec. M.

a. When the fierce north wind, with his airy forces, Rears up the Baltic to a foaming fury; And the red lightning, with a storm of hail, comes Rushing amain down.

8. Stop here, my fancy; (all away, ye horrid Doleful ideas,) come, arise to Jesus, How he sits God-like! and the saints around him Thron'd, yet adoring,

Loud.   Moderate.   LANCASTER. 7s

Rushing amain down.   1. Christ the Lord is risen to day, Sons of men and angels say; Raise your joys and triumphs high, Sing ye heavens, and earth reply.

Thron'd, yet ador - ing.   2. Loves redeeming work is done, Fought the fight, the battle won; Lo! our sun's eclipse is o'er, Lo! he sets in blood no more.

Slow & solemn.   DUNBAR. S. M. Soft.   Loud.

Gb [music staff]

And will the Judge descend, And must the dead a - rise, And not a sin - gle soul escape His all discern - ing eyes?

Gb [music staff]

Gb [music staff]

Fb [music staff]

Moderate.   AUGUSTA. C. M.

Gb [music staff]

With joy we medi - tate the grace Of our High Priest above; His heart is made of tenderness, His bowels melt with love.

Gb [music staff]

Gb [music staff]

Fb [music staff]

HABAKKUK. L. M. Soft.

1. Away, my un - be - liev - ing fear! Fear shall in me no more take place! My Saviour doth not yet ap - pear, He hides the

2. Barren although my soul remain, And not one bud of grace appear, No fruit of all my toil and pain, But sin, and

Loud.

brightness of his face; But shall I therefore let him go, And basely to the tempter yield? No; in the strength of Jesus, no; I never will give

on - ly sin is here; Altho' my gifts and comforts lost, My blooming hopes cut off I see, Yet will I in my Saviour trust, Whose matchless grace ca up my shield. Altho' the vine its fruit deny, 'Altho' the olive yield no oil, The withering fig tree droop and die, The field illude the tiller's

reach to me. In hope, believing against hope, His promis'd mercy will I claim; His gracious word shall bear me up, To seek salva - tion in his

Loud.

toil; The empty stall no herd afford, And perish, all the bleating race; Yet will I triumph in the Lord, The God of my salvation praise.

name; Soon, my dear Saviour, bring it nigh; My soul shall then out strip the wind; On wings of love mount up on high, And leave the world and sin behind.

HAVERHILL. L. M.

I waited patient for the Lord; Who did his gracious ear afford; He bow'd to hear my humble cry; His goodness brought salvation

Unisons.   Unisons.

nigh, He rais'd me from a horrid pit, And from my bonds released my feet; Firm on a rock he made me stand, To praise the wonders of his hand.

OLIVET. Pec. M.

1. Sweet the moments rich in blessing, Which be - fore the cross I spend, Life and health and peace possessing, From the sinner's dy - ing

2. Far above yon glorious ceiling Of the a - zure vaulted sky, Jesus sits his grace re - vealing To the splended troops on

friend. Here I'll sit, for ever viewing Mercy's streams in streams of blood; Precious drops my soul bedewing Plead and claim my peace with God.

high. Hosts se - raphic humbly bowing, At his footstool prostrate fall; Saints and angels all a - vowing, God in Christ their all in all.

SHEFFIELD.

Sinner, O why so thoughtless grown? Why in such dreadful haste to die? Daring to leap to worlds unknown, Heedless against thy God to fly?

Sinner, O why so thoughtless grown? Why in such dreadful haste to die? Daring to leap to worlds unknown, Heedless against thy God to fly?

Wilt thou despise e - ternal fate, Urg'd on by sin's fantas - tic dreams, Madly attempt th', infer - nal gate, And force thy pas - sage to the flames?

Wilt thou despise 'e - ternal fate, Urg'd on by sin's fantas - tic dreams, Madly attempt th' infer - nal gate, And force thy pas - sage to the flames?

stay, stay, stay sinner stay, stay sinner on the gospel plains, Behold, behold the God of love unfold, The glories of his dying pains, For

stay, stay, stay sinner stay, stay sinner on the gospel plains, Behold, behold the God of love unfold, The glories of his dying pains, For

slow.

ever telling, yet untold, for ever, for ever, for ever telling, ever telling, yet untold, for ever telling, ever telling, yet untold.

ever telling, yet untold, for ever, for ever, for ever telling, ever telling, yet untold, for ever telling, ever telling, yet untold.

AVON.

At an - chor laid re - mote from home, Tolling I cry sweet Spi - rit come, Tolling I cry sweet Spi - rit come, Ce - lest - ial breeze

At an - chor laid re - mote from home, Tolling I cry sweet Spi - rit come, Tolling I cry sweet Spi - rit come, Ce - lest - ial breeze

no longer stay; But swell my sails, and speed my way, But swell my sails and speed my way, Fain would I mount, fain would I glow; Fain would I mount, fain would I

no longer stay; But swell my sails and speed my way, Fain would I mount, fain would I

But swell my sails and speed my way,

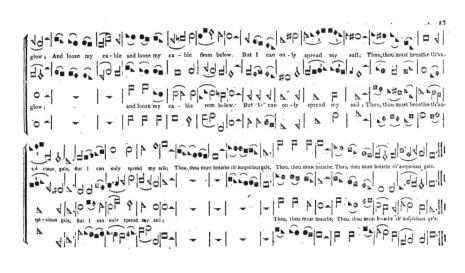

glow; And loose my ca - ble and loose my ca - ble from below. But I can on - ly spread my sail; Thou, thou must breathe th'au-

glow; and loose my ca - ble rom below. But I can on - ly spread my sail; Thou, thou must breathe th'au-

spi - cious gale, But I can only spread my sail; Thou, thou must breathe th'auspicious gale, Thou, thou must breathe, Thou, thou must breathe th' auspicious gale.

spi - cious gale, But I can only spread my sail; Thou, thou must breathe, Thou, thou must breathe th' auspicious gale.

NEW YORK. Slow and Soft. Increase.

Vital spark of heavenly flame; Quit, Oh quit this mortal frame, Trembling, hoping, ling'ring, flying, Oh the pain, the bliss of dying!

Vital spark of heavenly flame; Quit, Oh quit this mortal frame, Oh the pain, the bliss of dying!

Slow and Soft. Increase. Cheerful. Soft.

Cease, fond nature, cease thy strife, and let me languish into life! Hark! they whisper, angels say, they whisper, angels say, Hark!

Hark!

And let me languish into life! Hark! Hark! Hark! they whisper angels say,

Loud. Soft.   Loud.   Modérate and Soft.

Hark! they whisper, angels say, Sister spirit come a-way! Sister spirit come away! What is this absorbs me quite? Steals my senses?

Hark! they whisper, angels say, Sister spirit come away! What is this absorbs me quite? Steals my senses?

Loud.   Soft.   Increase.   Slow.   Moderate. Soft.

shuts my sight? Drowns my spirits? draws my breath? Tell me my soul, can this be death? Tell me my soul, can this be death? The world recedes; it

shuts my sight? Drowns my spirits? draws my breath? Tell me my soul, can this be death? Tell me my soul, can this be death? The world recedes; it

Increase. Loud. Diminish. Increase.   Cheerful.

dis - appears; Heaven opens on my eyes! My ears with sounds seraph - ic ring,   Lend, lend your wings, I mount, I fly, O grave, where is thy victory! O

dis - appears; Heaven opens on my eyes! My ears with sounds seraph - ic ring.   Lend, lend your wings, I mount, I fly, O grave, where is thy victory! O

Soft.

grave, where is thy vic - to - ry; O death, where is thy sting ! O grave, where is thy victory ! O death, where is thy sting ! Lend, lend your wings, I mount, I

grave, where is thy vic - to - ry, O death where is thy sting ! O grave, where is thy victory ! O death, where is thy sting ! Lend, lend your wings, I mount, I

fly, O grave, where is thy vic-to-ry, thy vic-to-ry! O grave, where is thy vic-to-ry, thy vic-to-ry! O death, where is thy sting! O death, where is thy sting!

fly, O grave, where is thy vic-to-ry, thy vic-to-ry! O grave, where is thy vic-to-ry, thy vic-to-ry! O death, where is thy sting! O death, where is thy sting!

Loud,

Very Slow.

Lend, lend your wings, I mount, I fly, I mount, I fly, O grave, where is thy vic-to-ry, thy vic-to-ry! O death, O death, where is thy sting!

Lend, lend your wings, I mount, I fly, I mount, I fly, O grave, where is thy vic-to-ry, thy vic-to-ry! O death, O death, where is thy sting!

88 Moderate.

The God of glory sends his summons forth, Calls the south nations and awakes the north; From east to west the sov'reign orders spread, Through distant worlds and re - gions of the dead. The trumpet sounds; hell trembles; heaven re - joices; Lift up your heads, ye saints, with cheerful voices.

Moderate.   Soft.

Praise ye the Lord; 'tis good to raise Our hearts and voices in his praise; Our hearts and voices in his praise. His nature and his works invite To make this duty our de-

Loud.   Moderate.   COOKHAM. 7s.

light. To make this du - ty our delight.   Now begin the heavenly theme Sing aloud in Je - su's name, Ye who Jesu's kindness prove, Triumph in redeeming love,

M

OPORTO. L. M.   Soft.

Moderate.

With all my powers of heart and tongue, I'll praise my Maker in my song. Angels shall hear the notes I raise, Approve the song, and join the

Loud.   Cheerful.   COLUMBIA. S. M.

praise. Approve the song, and join the praise.   My God, my life, my love, To thee, to thee I call; I cannot live if thou remove, For thou art all in all.

TRANSPORT. L. M.

Give thanks to God; he reigns above, Kind are his thoughts, his name is love; Kind are his thoughts His mercy ages past have known, And ages long to come shall

GILBOA. S. M.

own, And ages long to come shall own. Exalt the Lord our God, And worship at his feet; His ways are wisdom, pow'r and truth, And mercy is his seat.

91

CARMEL. L. M.

Moderate.

The Lord, how wond'rous are his ways! How firm his truth, how large his grace! He takes his mercy for his throne, And thence he makes his

GILGAL. L. M.

Moderate.

glo-ries known.

Sweet is the work, my God, my King, To praise thy name, give thanks and sing: To show thy love by morning light, And talk of all thy truth at night.

Moderate.

ARMLEY. L. M.

Stay, thou insult-ed Spi-rit, stay, Tho' I have done thee such despite, Nor cast the sin-ner quite away, Nor take thine ever-

Moderate.

BETHEL. C. M.

lasting flight.

This is the day the Lord hath made, He calls the hours his own, Let heaven rejoice, let earth be glad, And praise surround the throne.

LAMBERTON. 8s. Pec.   Loud.

Cheerful.   Soft.

Thou Shepherd of Israel, and mine, The joy and desire of my heart, For closer communion I pine, I long to reside where thou art: The pasture I

Soft.   Loud.   Moderate.   NEWCOURT. L. M.

languish to find, Where all who the's shepherd obey, Are fed, on thy bosom reclin'd, And screen'd from the heat of the day.

Come, let our voices join to raise, A

sacred song of solemn praise; A sa-cred song of solemn praise; God is a sovereign King; rehearse His honor in exalted verse. His honor in exalted verse.

DAMASCUS. C. M.

My God, the spring of all my joys, The life of my delights, The glory of my brightest days, And comfort of my nights! And comfort of my nights!

Soft. **GLOCESTER.** L. M. Loud.

96 Moderate.

Th' Almighty reigns, exalted high O'er all the earth, o'er all the sky: Tho' clouds and darkness veil his feet, His dwelling is the mercy seat. Tho' clouds and darkness

Slow. **ORLEANS.** 5. 11.

veil his feet, His dwelling is the mercy seat. . . . All ye that pass by, To Jesus draw nigh: To you is it nothing that Jesus should die?

Moderate.

SWANICK, C.M.

, Lord, thou wilt hear me when I pray; I am for ev - er thine; I fear before thee all the day, Nor would I dare to sin, Nor would I

Moderate.

BREWER. L.M.

dare to sin.   Thou, whom my soul admires above All earthly joy and earthly love, Tell me, dear Shepherd, let me know Where do thy sweetest pastures grow?

N

Unisons.

98 Cheerful.

Rejoice, the Lord is King, Your Lord and King adore; Mortals, give thanks, and sing, And tri - umph ev - er - more! Lift up the

Moderate. ELENBOROUGH. C. M.

heart, lift up the voice, Rejoice' a - loud, ye saints, rejoice!

How vain are all things here below! How false, and yet how fair! Each pleasure hath its poi - son too, Each pleasure hath its poi - son too, And eve - ry sweet a snare, And eve - ry sweet a snare.

PECKHAM. S. M.

Al - migh - ty Maker, God! How wond'rous is thy name! Thy glories how diffused a - broad Thro' the cre - ation's frame.

KINGSBRIDGE. L. M.

Moderate.

Great God, indulge my humble claim, Thou art my hope, my joy, my rest; The glories that compose thy name Stand all engag'd to make me blest.

DUMAH. C. M.

Moderate.

My drowsy powers, why sleep ye so! Awake, my sluggish soul! Nothing has half thy work to do; Yet nothing's half so dull!

Moderate.   CASTLE STREET. L. M.   Loud. 101

Again, my tongue, thy silence break, My heart and all my powers, awake; My tongue, the glory of my frame, Awake, and sing Jehovah's name, Awake, and sing

Cheerful.   STAUGHTON. C. M.

Je - ho - vah's name,   There is a land of pure delight, Where saints immortal reign; Infin - ite day excludes the night, And pleasures banish pain.

WARSAW. 10s.

In boundless mercy, gracious Lord appear, Darkness dispel, the humble mourner cheer; Vain thoughts remove, melt down this flinty heart; Cause every soul to choose the

Moderate. TYGRIS. S. M.

better part. Blest are the sons of peace, Whose hearts and hopes are one, Whose kind designs to serve and please Thro' all their actions run.

Moderate.   B E A U F O R T. 7: 8.

G♭ ⊃ P

Head of the church triumphant, We joyful - ly adore thee; Till thou appear, thy members here Shall sing like those in glory, Shall sing like those in

G♭ ⊃

G♭ ⊃ P

F♭ ⊃ P

glory. We lift our hearts and voices, With blest anticipa - tion; And cry aloud, cry aloud, cry aloud, and give to God, And cry aloud, and give to God The praise of our salvation.

104 Moderate.

COOS. 8. 4.

Hark ! how the gospel trumpet founds ! Thro' all the earth the echo bounds ! And Jesus, by redeeming blood, Is bringing sinners back to God ; And guides them safely

Moderate.

GILEAD. 7s.

by his word To endless day. Children of the heavenly King, As ye journey, sweetly sing ; Sing your Saviour's worthy praise, Glorious in his works and ways.

Cheerful.

AMSTERDAM. 7. 6. 7.

Rise my soul and stretch thy wings, Thy better portion trace; Sun and moon and stars decay, Time shall soon this earth remove; To seats prepared above.
Rise from transitory things, Tow'rds heaven thy native place. Rise my soul, and haste away.

Moderate.

PETERSBURG. S.M.

And must this bo - dy die? This mortal frame decay; And must these active limbs of mine Lie mould'ring in the clay? Lie mould'ring in the clay.

O

Cheerful.   MEDWAY 7. 6.

O when shall I see Jesus, And reign with him above; And reign with him above And from that flowing fountain Drink everlasting love? Drink everlast-

When shall I be deliver'd From this vain world of sin ; From this vain world of sin ; And with my blessed Jesus, Drink endless pleasures in ? Drink endless pleas-

Moderate.   SWEDESBORO. S. M.

ing love?   1. Raise your triumphant songs, To an immor - tal tune : Let the wide earth resound the deeds Ce - lest - ial grace has done.

sures in ?   2. Sing how e - ter - nal love Its chief beloved chose, And bade 'him raise our wretched race From their abyss of woes.

Unisons. BURTON. P. M.

To bless the Lord let every land combine ; Your hearts and minds, your harps and voices join. Each opening dawn shall hear my songs arise ;

Each evening waft its incense to the skies, .   All praise, all love, his boundless glories claim,   The praise of saints, the seraphs sacred flame.

Moderate.

Ex - alt - ed high, at God's right hand, Near - er the throne than cherubs stand, With glory crown'd in bright ar-

Ex - alt - ed high, at God's right hand, Near - er the throne than cherubs stand, With glory crown'd in bright ar-

ray, My wond' - - - - ring soul says who are they? who are they? My wond' - - - - ring soul says who are they?

ray, My wond' - ring wond'ring soul says who are they? who are they? . My wond' - ring won l'ring soul says who are they?

116   Soft. Treble and Bass.

These are the saints, belov'd of God, Wash'd are their robes in Jesu's blood; More spotless than the

purest white, More spotless than the purest white, They shine in un - cre - a - ted light, They shine in un - cre - a - ted light,

Loud.

Amen, amen, amen, amen they cry to him alone, Who dares to fill his Fathers throne. They give him glory, they give him glory,

Soft.

Amen, amen, amen, amen they cry to him alone, Who dares to fill his Father's throne. They give him glory, they give him glory, his praise and say a - men, a - men.

a - - men, a - - men, a - men, a - men, a - men,

his praise and say a - men, a - - - - men, a - - - - men, a - men,

Slow.

him glory, and again, Repeat his praise, Repeat his praise, and say a - men.

him glory, and again, Repeat his praise, Repeat his praise, and say a - men,

Abridge	C	42	Carmel	L	92	Gilgal	L	92	Miletus	L	89	Surry	L
Amsterdam	7, 6, 7	105	Carr's Lane	C	38	Glocester	L	96	Mill Ville	Pec.	64	Sutton	S
Arabia	C	107	Castle Street	L	101	Groton	L	18	Milton	C	34	Swanick	C
Archdale	C	53	Chapel	P	58	Haddam	S	31	Myra	S	70	Swedesboro	S 100
Armley	L	93	Charleston	P	30	Hamburg	S	37	Naples	C	36	Tempest	Pec. 74
Ashley	C	56	Colchester	C	24	Hanover	Pec.	32	Nantwich	L	41	Transport	L 91
Athens	C	51	Columbia	S	90	Haverhill	L	78	Neston	L	29	Trinity	Pec. 55
Augusta	C	75	Concord	L	53	Hotham	P	46	Newcourt	L	94	Turin	P. 62
Aylesbury	S	18	Cookham	7s.	89	Irish	C	13	New London	L	24	Tygris	S. 102
			Coos	8, 4.	104	Islington	L		Norfolk	C	14	Vienna	P 58
Bangor	C	40	Coventry	S	91	Italy	L.	57	Norwich	Pec.	66	Wakefield	C 23
Beaufort	7, 8.	103	Damascus	C	95	Jerusalem	P	48	Old 100	L	42	Walsal	C 40
Bedford	C	16	Derby	C	69	Judea	C	98	Olivet	Pec.	79	Warren	P 88
Berea	C	63	Dublin	C	17	Kingsbridge	L	65	Oporto	L	90	Warsaw	10s. 102
Bethel	C	93	Dumah	C	100			100	Orleans	5, 11.	96	Whitfield	S 38
Bethesda	P	25	Dunbar	S	75	Lamberton	8s. Pec.	94	Peckham	S		Winchester	Pec. 54
Bethlehem	S	21	Dunstan	L	22	Lancaster	7s.	74	Pelham	S	99	Windsor	C 73
Beverly	S	13				Lebanon	L	54	Petersburg		34	Woodbury	C 39
Bloomfield	S	20	Easton		28	Leeds	L	27	Portland	S	105		
Bolton	L	15	Elenborough	C	98	Leoni	P.	68	Portsmouth	P	52		
Brewer	P	97	Ephesus	C	71	Litchfield	L	21	Portugal	L.	72	**PIECES.**	
Bristol	Pec.	73	Evening Hy.	L	67	Lystra	P	70	Putney	L.	22	Avon	82
Broomsgrove	C	107	Falmouth	P	43	Malden	C	41	Reading	C	19	Funeral Piece	49
Burford	C	35	Galilee	Pec.	64	Malta	Pec.	62	Scotland	S	25	Habakkuk	76
Burton	P	108	Gath	L	26	Mansfield	S	32	Sicily	C	29	Kedron	60
Cadiz	P	50	Germany	S	28	Marseilles	P.	66	Southbury	P	57	New York	84
Calvary	Pec	68	Georgia	C	20	Mear	C	14	Stamford	Pec.	26	Sheffield	80
Cambridge	C	59	Gilboa	S	91	Medway	7, 6.	106	Staughton	C	47	Washington	44
Canton	P	36	Gilead	7s.	104	Milan	C	13	Sunderland	P	101	Woodstock	109

N. B. The Metres are designated by the letters which are placed after the names of the tunes in the index. L. shows that the tune is long metre. C. common metre; S. short metre; and P. particular metre.

INDEX.

Tune	Metre	No.
Abridge	C	42
Amsterdam	7, 6, ⅄	105
Arabia	C	107
Archdale	C	53
Armley	L	93
Ashley	C	56
Athens	C	51
Augusta	C	75
Aylesbury	S	18
Bangor	C	40
Beaufort	7, 8.	103
Bedford	C	16
Berea	C	63
Bethel	C	93
Bethesda	P	25
Bethlehem	S	21
Beverly		13
Bloomfield	S	20
Bolton	L	15
Brewer	L	97
Bristol	Pec.	73
Broomsgrove	C	107
Burford	C	55
Burton	P	108
Cadiz	P	50
Calvary	Pec	68
Cambridge	C	59
Canton	P	36
Carmel	L	92
Carr's Lane	C	38
Castle Street	L	101
Chapel	P	58
Charleston	P	30
Colchester	C	24
Columbia	S	90
Concord	L	53
Cookham	7s.	89
Coos	8, 4.	104
Coventry	S	91
Damascus	C	95
Derby	C	69
Dublin	C	17
Dumah	C	100
Dunbar	S	75
Dunstan	L	22
Easton		28
Elenborough	C	98
Ephesus	C	71
Evening Hy.	L	67
Falmouth	P	43
Galilee	Pec.	64
Gath	L	26
Germany	S	28
Georgia	C	20
Gilboa	S	91
Gilead	7s.	104
Gilgal	L	92
Glocester	L	96
Groton	L	18
Haddam	S	31
Hamburg	S	37
Hanover	Pec.	32
Haverhill	L	78
Hotham	P	46
Irish	C	13
Islington	L	57
Italy	I.	48
Jerusalem	P	98
Judea	C	65
Kingsbridge	L	100
Lamberton	8s. Pec.	94
Lancaster	7s.	74
Lebanon	L	54
Leeds	L	27
Leoni	P.	68
Litchfield	L	21
Lystra	P	70
Malden	C	41
Malta	Pec.	62
Mansfield	S	32
Marseilles	P.	66
Mear	C	14
Medway	7, 6.	106
Milan	C	13
Miletus	L	89
Mill Ville	Pec.	64
Milton	C	34
Myra	S	70
Naples	C	36
Nantwich	L	41
Neston	L	29
Newcourt	L	94
New London	L	24
Norfolk	C	14
Norwich	Pec.	66
Old 100	L	42
Olivet	Pec.	79
Oporto	L	90
Orleans	5, 11.	
Peckham	S	96
Pelham	S	99
Petersburg	S	34
Portland	S	52
Portsmouth	P	72
Portugal	L	22
Putney	L	19
Reading	C	25
Scotland	L	29
Sicily	C	57
Southbury	P	26
Stamford	Pec.	47
Staughton	C	101
Sunderland	P	30
Surry	L	23
Sutton	S	16
Swanick	C	97
Swedesboro	S	106
Tempest	Pec.	74
Transport	L	91
Trinity	Pec.	55
Turin	P.	62
Tygris	S.	102
Vienna	P	58
Wakefield	C	23
Walsal	C	40
Warren	P	88
Warsaw	10s.	102
Whitfield	S	38
Winchester	Pec.	54
Windsor	C	73
Woodbury	C	39

PIECES.

Piece	No.
Avon	82
Funeral Piece	49
Habakkuk	76
Kedron	60
New York	84
Sheffield	80
Washington	44
Woodstock	109

N. B. The Metres are designated by the letters which are placed after the names of the tunes in the index. L. shows that the tune is long metre. C. common metre; S. short metre; and P. particular metre.